Personal Information

Name:

Address:

Email:

Cell Phone:

Home Phone:

Work Phone:

Emergency Numbers

Police:

Fire Department:

Doctor:

Local Hospital:

Animal Control:

Emergency Contact #1:

Emergency Contact #2:

Emergency Contact #3:

Name:		
Street Address:		
City:	State:	Zip Code:
Home Phone:		Cell Phone:
Work Phone:		Email:

Name:		
Street Address:		
City:	State:	Zip Code:
Home Phone:		Cell Phone:
Work Phone:		Email:

Name:		
Street Address:		
City:	State:	Zip Code:
Home Phone:		Cell Phone:
Work Phone:		Email:

Name:		
Street Address:		
City:	State:	Zip Code:
Home Phone:		Cell Phone:
Work Phone:		Email:

A

Name:		
Street Address:		
City:	State:	Zip Code:
Home Phone:		Cell Phone:
Work Phone:		Email:

Name:		
Street Address:		
City:	State:	Zip Code:
Home Phone:		Cell Phone:
Work Phone:		Email:

Name:		
Street Address:		
City:	State:	Zip Code:
Home Phone:		Cell Phone:
Work Phone:		Email:

Name:		
Street Address:		
City:	State:	Zip Code:
Home Phone:		Cell Phone:
Work Phone:		Email:

Name:		
Street Address:		
City:	State:	Zip Code:
Home Phone:		Cell Phone:
Work Phone:		Email:

Name:		
Street Address:		
City:	State:	Zip Code:
Home Phone:		Cell Phone:
Work Phone:		Email:

Name:		
Street Address:		
City:	State:	Zip Code:
Home Phone:		Cell Phone:
Work Phone:		Email:

Name:		
Street Address:		
City:	State:	Zip Code:
Home Phone:		Cell Phone:
Work Phone:		Email:

A

Name:		
Street Address:		
City:	State:	Zip Code:
Home Phone:		Cell Phone:
Work Phone:		Email:

Name:		
Street Address:		
City:	State:	Zip Code:
Home Phone:		Cell Phone:
Work Phone:		Email:

Name:		
Street Address:		
City:	State:	Zip Code:
Home Phone:		Cell Phone:
Work Phone:		Email:

Name:		
Street Address:		
City:	State:	Zip Code:
Home Phone:		Cell Phone:
Work Phone:		Email:

Name:		
Street Address:		
City:	State:	Zip Code:
Home Phone:		Cell Phone:
Work Phone:		Email:

Name:		
Street Address:		
City:	State:	Zip Code:
Home Phone:		Cell Phone:
Work Phone:		Email:

Name:		
Street Address:		
City:	State:	Zip Code:
Home Phone:		Cell Phone:
Work Phone:		Email:

Name:		
Street Address:		
City:	State:	Zip Code:
Home Phone:		Cell Phone:
Work Phone:		Email:

A

Name:		
Street Address:		
City:	State:	Zip Code:
Home Phone:		Cell Phone:
Work Phone:		Email:

Name:		
Street Address:		
City:	State:	Zip Code:
Home Phone:		Cell Phone:
Work Phone:		Email:

Name:		
Street Address:		
City:	State:	Zip Code:
Home Phone:		Cell Phone:
Work Phone:		Email:

Name:		
Street Address:		
City:	State:	Zip Code:
Home Phone:		Cell Phone:
Work Phone:		Email:

B

<table>
<tr><td>Name:</td><td></td><td></td></tr>
<tr><td colspan="3">Street Address:</td></tr>
<tr><td>City:</td><td>State:</td><td>Zip Code:</td></tr>
<tr><td colspan="2">Home Phone:</td><td>Cell Phone:</td></tr>
<tr><td colspan="2">Work Phone:</td><td>Email:</td></tr>
</table>

<table>
<tr><td>Name:</td><td></td><td></td></tr>
<tr><td colspan="3">Street Address:</td></tr>
<tr><td>City:</td><td>State:</td><td>Zip Code:</td></tr>
<tr><td colspan="2">Home Phone:</td><td>Cell Phone:</td></tr>
<tr><td colspan="2">Work Phone:</td><td>Email:</td></tr>
</table>

<table>
<tr><td>Name:</td><td></td><td></td></tr>
<tr><td colspan="3">Street Address:</td></tr>
<tr><td>City:</td><td>State:</td><td>Zip Code:</td></tr>
<tr><td colspan="2">Home Phone:</td><td>Cell Phone:</td></tr>
<tr><td colspan="2">Work Phone:</td><td>Email:</td></tr>
</table>

<table>
<tr><td>Name:</td><td></td><td></td></tr>
<tr><td colspan="3">Street Address:</td></tr>
<tr><td>City:</td><td>State:</td><td>Zip Code:</td></tr>
<tr><td colspan="2">Home Phone:</td><td>Cell Phone:</td></tr>
<tr><td colspan="2">Work Phone:</td><td>Email:</td></tr>
</table>

B

Name:		
Street Address:		
City:	State:	Zip Code:
Home Phone:		Cell Phone:
Work Phone:		Email:

Name:		
Street Address:		
City:	State:	Zip Code:
Home Phone:		Cell Phone:
Work Phone:		Email:

Name:		
Street Address:		
City:	State:	Zip Code:
Home Phone:		Cell Phone:
Work Phone:		Email:

Name:		
Street Address:		
City:	State:	Zip Code:
Home Phone:		Cell Phone:
Work Phone:		Email:

B

Name:		
Street Address:		
City:	State:	Zip Code:
Home Phone:		Cell Phone:
Work Phone:		Email:

Name:		
Street Address:		
City:	State:	Zip Code:
Home Phone:		Cell Phone:
Work Phone:		Email:

Name:		
Street Address:		
City:	State:	Zip Code:
Home Phone:		Cell Phone:
Work Phone:		Email:

Name:		
Street Address:		
City:	State:	Zip Code:
Home Phone:		Cell Phone:
Work Phone:		Email:

B

Name:		
Street Address:		
City:	State:	Zip Code:
Home Phone:		Cell Phone:
Work Phone:		Email:

Name:		
Street Address:		
City:	State:	Zip Code:
Home Phone:		Cell Phone:
Work Phone:		Email:

Name:		
Street Address:		
City:	State:	Zip Code:
Home Phone:		Cell Phone:
Work Phone:		Email:

Name:		
Street Address:		
City:	State:	Zip Code:
Home Phone:		Cell Phone:
Work Phone:		Email:

B

Name:		
Street Address:		
City:	State:	Zip Code:
Home Phone:		Cell Phone:
Work Phone:		Email:

Name:		
Street Address:		
City:	State:	Zip Code:
Home Phone:		Cell Phone:
Work Phone:		Email:

Name:		
Street Address:		
City:	State:	Zip Code:
Home Phone:		Cell Phone:
Work Phone:		Email:

Name:		
Street Address:		
City:	State:	Zip Code:
Home Phone:		Cell Phone:
Work Phone:		Email:

B

Name:		
Street Address:		
City:	State:	Zip Code:
Home Phone:		Cell Phone:
Work Phone:		Email:

Name:		
Street Address:		
City:	State:	Zip Code:
Home Phone:		Cell Phone:
Work Phone:		Email:

Name:		
Street Address:		
City:	State:	Zip Code:
Home Phone:		Cell Phone:
Work Phone:		Email:

Name:		
Street Address:		
City:	State:	Zip Code:
Home Phone:		Cell Phone:
Work Phone:		Email:

Name:		
Street Address:		
City:	State:	Zip Code:
Home Phone:		Cell Phone:
Work Phone:		Email:

Name:		
Street Address:		
City:	State:	Zip Code:
Home Phone:		Cell Phone:
Work Phone:		Email:

Name:		
Street Address:		
City:	State:	Zip Code:
Home Phone:		Cell Phone:
Work Phone:		Email:

Name:		
Street Address:		
City:	State:	Zip Code:
Home Phone:		Cell Phone:
Work Phone:		Email:

C

Name:		
Street Address:		
City:	State:	Zip Code:
Home Phone:		Cell Phone:
Work Phone:		Email:

Name:		
Street Address:		
City:	State:	Zip Code:
Home Phone:		Cell Phone:
Work Phone:		Email:

Name:		
Street Address:		
City:	State:	Zip Code:
Home Phone:		Cell Phone:
Work Phone:		Email:

Name:		
Street Address:		
City:	State:	Zip Code:
Home Phone:		Cell Phone:
Work Phone:		Email:

Name:		
Street Address:		
City:	State:	Zip Code:
Home Phone:		Cell Phone:
Work Phone:		Email:

Name:		
Street Address:		
City:	State:	Zip Code:
Home Phone:		Cell Phone:
Work Phone:		Email:

Name:		
Street Address:		
City:	State:	Zip Code:
Home Phone:		Cell Phone:
Work Phone:		Email:

Name:		
Street Address:		
City:	State:	Zip Code:
Home Phone:		Cell Phone:
Work Phone:		Email:

C

Name:		
Street Address:		
City:	State:	Zip Code:
Home Phone:		Cell Phone:
Work Phone:		Email:

Name:		
Street Address:		
City:	State:	Zip Code:
Home Phone:		Cell Phone:
Work Phone:		Email:

Name:		
Street Address:		
City:	State:	Zip Code:
Home Phone:		Cell Phone:
Work Phone:		Email:

Name:		
Street Address:		
City:	State:	Zip Code:
Home Phone:		Cell Phone:
Work Phone:		Email:

Name:		
Street Address:		
City:	State:	Zip Code:
Home Phone:		Cell Phone:
Work Phone:		Email:

Name:		
Street Address:		
City:	State:	Zip Code:
Home Phone:		Cell Phone:
Work Phone:		Email:

Name:		
Street Address:		
City:	State:	Zip Code:
Home Phone:		Cell Phone:
Work Phone:		Email:

Name:		
Street Address:		
City:	State:	Zip Code:
Home Phone:		Cell Phone:
Work Phone:		Email:

D

Name:		
Street Address:		
City:	State:	Zip Code:
Home Phone:		Cell Phone:
Work Phone:		Email:

Name:		
Street Address:		
City:	State:	Zip Code:
Home Phone:		Cell Phone:
Work Phone:		Email:

Name:		
Street Address:		
City:	State:	Zip Code:
Home Phone:		Cell Phone:
Work Phone:		Email:

Name:		
Street Address:		
City:	State:	Zip Code:
Home Phone:		Cell Phone:
Work Phone:		Email:

Name:		
Street Address:		
City:	State:	Zip Code:
Home Phone:		Cell Phone:
Work Phone:		Email:

Name:		
Street Address:		
City:	State:	Zip Code:
Home Phone:		Cell Phone:
Work Phone:		Email:

Name:		
Street Address:		
City:	State:	Zip Code:
Home Phone:		Cell Phone:
Work Phone:		Email:

Name:		
Street Address:		
City:	State:	Zip Code:
Home Phone:		Cell Phone:
Work Phone:		Email:

D

Name:		
Street Address:		
City:	State:	Zip Code:
Home Phone:		Cell Phone:
Work Phone:		Email:

Name:		
Street Address:		
City:	State:	Zip Code:
Home Phone:		Cell Phone:
Work Phone:		Email:

Name:		
Street Address:		
City:	State:	Zip Code:
Home Phone:		Cell Phone:
Work Phone:		Email:

Name:		
Street Address:		
City:	State:	Zip Code:
Home Phone:		Cell Phone:
Work Phone:		Email:

E

Name:		
Street Address:		
City:	State:	Zip Code:
Home Phone:	Cell Phone:	
Work Phone:	Email:	

Name:		
Street Address:		
City:	State:	Zip Code:
Home Phone:	Cell Phone:	
Work Phone:	Email:	

Name:		
Street Address:		
City:	State:	Zip Code:
Home Phone:	Cell Phone:	
Work Phone:	Email:	

Name:		
Street Address:		
City:	State:	Zip Code:
Home Phone:	Cell Phone:	
Work Phone:	Email:	

E

Name:		
Street Address:		
City:	State:	Zip Code:
Home Phone:		Cell Phone:
Work Phone:		Email:

Name:		
Street Address:		
City:	State:	Zip Code:
Home Phone:		Cell Phone:
Work Phone:		Email:

Name:		
Street Address:		
City:	State:	Zip Code:
Home Phone:		Cell Phone:
Work Phone:		Email:

Name:		
Street Address:		
City:	State:	Zip Code:
Home Phone:		Cell Phone:
Work Phone:		Email:

E

Name:		
Street Address:		
City:	State:	Zip Code:
Home Phone:		Cell Phone:
Work Phone:		Email:

Name:		
Street Address:		
City:	State:	Zip Code:
Home Phone:		Cell Phone:
Work Phone:		Email:

Name:		
Street Address:		
City:	State:	Zip Code:
Home Phone:		Cell Phone:
Work Phone:		Email:

Name:		
Street Address:		
City:	State:	Zip Code:
Home Phone:		Cell Phone:
Work Phone:		Email:

E

Name:		
Street Address:		
City:	State:	Zip Code:
Home Phone:		Cell Phone:
Work Phone:		Email:

Name:		
Street Address:		
City:	State:	Zip Code:
Home Phone:		Cell Phone:
Work Phone:		Email:

Name:		
Street Address:		
City:	State:	Zip Code:
Home Phone:		Cell Phone:
Work Phone:		Email:

Name:		
Street Address:		
City:	State:	Zip Code:
Home Phone:		Cell Phone:
Work Phone:		Email:

Name:		
Street Address:		
City:	State:	Zip Code:
Home Phone:		Cell Phone:
Work Phone:		Email:

Name:		
Street Address:		
City:	State:	Zip Code:
Home Phone:		Cell Phone:
Work Phone:		Email:

Name:		
Street Address:		
City:	State:	Zip Code:
Home Phone:		Cell Phone:
Work Phone:		Email:

Name:		
Street Address:		
City:	State:	Zip Code:
Home Phone:		Cell Phone:
Work Phone:		Email:

F

Name:		
Street Address:		
City:	State:	Zip Code:
Home Phone:		Cell Phone:
Work Phone:		Email:

Name:		
Street Address:		
City:	State:	Zip Code:
Home Phone:		Cell Phone:
Work Phone:		Email:

Name:		
Street Address:		
City:	State:	Zip Code:
Home Phone:		Cell Phone:
Work Phone:		Email:

Name:		
Street Address:		
City:	State:	Zip Code:
Home Phone:		Cell Phone:
Work Phone:		Email:

F

Name:		
Street Address:		
City:	State:	Zip Code:
Home Phone:		Cell Phone:
Work Phone:		Email:

Name:		
Street Address:		
City:	State:	Zip Code:
Home Phone:		Cell Phone:
Work Phone:		Email:

Name:		
Street Address:		
City:	State:	Zip Code:
Home Phone:		Cell Phone:
Work Phone:		Email:

Name:		
Street Address:		
City:	State:	Zip Code:
Home Phone:		Cell Phone:
Work Phone:		Email:

F

Name:		
Street Address:		
City:	State:	Zip Code:
Home Phone:		Cell Phone:
Work Phone:		Email:

Name:		
Street Address:		
City:	State:	Zip Code:
Home Phone:		Cell Phone:
Work Phone:		Email:

Name:		
Street Address:		
City:	State:	Zip Code:
Home Phone:		Cell Phone:
Work Phone:		Email:

Name:		
Street Address:		
City:	State:	Zip Code:
Home Phone:		Cell Phone:
Work Phone:		Email:

Name:		
Street Address:		
City:	State:	Zip Code:
Home Phone:		Cell Phone:
Work Phone:		Email:

Name:		
Street Address:		
City:	State:	Zip Code:
Home Phone:		Cell Phone:
Work Phone:		Email:

Name:		
Street Address:		
City:	State:	Zip Code:
Home Phone:		Cell Phone:
Work Phone:		Email:

Name:		
Street Address:		
City:	State:	Zip Code:
Home Phone:		Cell Phone:
Work Phone:		Email:

G

Name:		
Street Address:		
City:	State:	Zip Code:
Home Phone:		Cell Phone:
Work Phone:		Email:

Name:		
Street Address:		
City:	State:	Zip Code:
Home Phone:		Cell Phone:
Work Phone:		Email:

Name:		
Street Address:		
City:	State:	Zip Code:
Home Phone:		Cell Phone:
Work Phone:		Email:

Name:		
Street Address:		
City:	State:	Zip Code:
Home Phone:		Cell Phone:
Work Phone:		Email:

Name:		
Street Address:		
City:	State:	Zip Code:
Home Phone:		Cell Phone:
Work Phone:		Email:

Name:		
Street Address:		
City:	State:	Zip Code:
Home Phone:		Cell Phone:
Work Phone:		Email:

Name:		
Street Address:		
City:	State:	Zip Code:
Home Phone:		Cell Phone:
Work Phone:		Email:

Name:		
Street Address:		
City:	State:	Zip Code:
Home Phone:		Cell Phone:
Work Phone:		Email:

G

Name:		
Street Address:		
City:	State:	Zip Code:
Home Phone:		Cell Phone:
Work Phone:		Email:

Name:		
Street Address:		
City:	State:	Zip Code:
Home Phone:		Cell Phone:
Work Phone:		Email:

Name:		
Street Address:		
City:	State:	Zip Code:
Home Phone:		Cell Phone:
Work Phone:		Email:

Name:		
Street Address:		
City:	State:	Zip Code:
Home Phone:		Cell Phone:
Work Phone:		Email:

Name:		
Street Address:		
City:	State:	Zip Code:
Home Phone:	Cell Phone:	
Work Phone:	Email:	

Name:		
Street Address:		
City:	State:	Zip Code:
Home Phone:	Cell Phone:	
Work Phone:	Email:	

Name:		
Street Address:		
City:	State:	Zip Code:
Home Phone:	Cell Phone:	
Work Phone:	Email:	

Name:		
Street Address:		
City:	State:	Zip Code:
Home Phone:	Cell Phone:	
Work Phone:	Email:	

H

Name:		
Street Address:		
City:	State:	Zip Code:
Home Phone:		Cell Phone:
Work Phone:		Email:

Name:		
Street Address:		
City:	State:	Zip Code:
Home Phone:		Cell Phone:
Work Phone:		Email:

Name:		
Street Address:		
City:	State:	Zip Code:
Home Phone:		Cell Phone:
Work Phone:		Email:

Name:		
Street Address:		
City:	State:	Zip Code:
Home Phone:		Cell Phone:
Work Phone:		Email:

Name:		
Street Address:		
City:	State:	Zip Code:
Home Phone:		Cell Phone:
Work Phone:		Email:

Name:		
Street Address:		
City:	State:	Zip Code:
Home Phone:		Cell Phone:
Work Phone:		Email:

Name:		
Street Address:		
City:	State:	Zip Code:
Home Phone:		Cell Phone:
Work Phone:		Email:

Name:		
Street Address:		
City:	State:	Zip Code:
Home Phone:		Cell Phone:
Work Phone:		Email:

H

Name:		
Street Address:		
City:	State:	Zip Code:
Home Phone:		Cell Phone:
Work Phone:		Email:

Name:		
Street Address:		
City:	State:	Zip Code:
Home Phone:		Cell Phone:
Work Phone:		Email:

Name:		
Street Address:		
City:	State:	Zip Code:
Home Phone:		Cell Phone:
Work Phone:		Email:

Name:		
Street Address:		
City:	State:	Zip Code:
Home Phone:		Cell Phone:
Work Phone:		Email:

H

Name:		
Street Address:		
City:	State:	Zip Code:
Home Phone:	Cell Phone:	
Work Phone:	Email:	

Name:		
Street Address:		
City:	State:	Zip Code:
Home Phone:	Cell Phone:	
Work Phone:	Email:	

Name:		
Street Address:		
City:	State:	Zip Code:
Home Phone:	Cell Phone:	
Work Phone:	Email:	

Name:		
Street Address:		
City:	State:	Zip Code:
Home Phone:	Cell Phone:	
Work Phone:	Email:	

H

Name:		
Street Address:		
City:	State:	Zip Code:
Home Phone:		Cell Phone:
Work Phone:		Email:

Name:		
Street Address:		
City:	State:	Zip Code:
Home Phone:		Cell Phone:
Work Phone:		Email:

Name:		
Street Address:		
City:	State:	Zip Code:
Home Phone:		Cell Phone:
Work Phone:		Email:

Name:		
Street Address:		
City:	State:	Zip Code:
Home Phone:		Cell Phone:
Work Phone:		Email:

Name:		
Street Address:		
City:	State:	Zip Code:
Home Phone:		Cell Phone:
Work Phone:		Email:

Name:		
Street Address:		
City:	State:	Zip Code:
Home Phone:		Cell Phone:
Work Phone:		Email:

Name:		
Street Address:		
City:	State:	Zip Code:
Home Phone:		Cell Phone:
Work Phone:		Email:

Name:		
Street Address:		
City:	State:	Zip Code:
Home Phone:		Cell Phone:
Work Phone:		Email:

Name:		
Street Address:		
City:	State:	Zip Code:
Home Phone:		Cell Phone:
Work Phone:		Email:

Name:		
Street Address:		
City:	State:	Zip Code:
Home Phone:		Cell Phone:
Work Phone:		Email:

Name:		
Street Address:		
City:	State:	Zip Code:
Home Phone:		Cell Phone:
Work Phone:		Email:

Name:		
Street Address:		
City:	State:	Zip Code:
Home Phone:		Cell Phone:
Work Phone:		Email:

Name:		
Street Address:		
City:	State:	Zip Code:
Home Phone:		Cell Phone:
Work Phone:		Email:

Name:		
Street Address:		
City:	State:	Zip Code:
Home Phone:		Cell Phone:
Work Phone:		Email:

Name:		
Street Address:		
City:	State:	Zip Code:
Home Phone:		Cell Phone:
Work Phone:		Email:

Name:		
Street Address:		
City:	State:	Zip Code:
Home Phone:		Cell Phone:
Work Phone:		Email:

Name:	
Street Address:	
City:	State:	Zip Code:
Home Phone:	Cell Phone:
Work Phone:	Email:

Name:	
Street Address:	
City:	State:	Zip Code:
Home Phone:	Cell Phone:
Work Phone:	Email:

Name:	
Street Address:	
City:	State:	Zip Code:
Home Phone:	Cell Phone:
Work Phone:	Email:

Name:	
Street Address:	
City:	State:	Zip Code:
Home Phone:	Cell Phone:
Work Phone:	Email:

Name:		
Street Address:		
City:	State:	Zip Code:
Home Phone:	Cell Phone:	
Work Phone:	Email:	

Name:		
Street Address:		
City:	State:	Zip Code:
Home Phone:	Cell Phone:	
Work Phone:	Email:	

Name:		
Street Address:		
City:	State:	Zip Code:
Home Phone:	Cell Phone:	
Work Phone:	Email:	

Name:		
Street Address:		
City:	State:	Zip Code:
Home Phone:	Cell Phone:	
Work Phone:	Email:	

I

Name:		
Street Address:		
City:	State:	Zip Code:
Home Phone:		Cell Phone:
Work Phone:		Email:

Name:		
Street Address:		
City:	State:	Zip Code:
Home Phone:		Cell Phone:
Work Phone:		Email:

Name:		
Street Address:		
City:	State:	Zip Code:
Home Phone:		Cell Phone:
Work Phone:		Email:

Name:		
Street Address:		
City:	State:	Zip Code:
Home Phone:		Cell Phone:
Work Phone:		Email:

J

Name:		
Street Address:		
City:	State:	Zip Code:
Home Phone:	Cell Phone:	
Work Phone:	Email:	

Name:		
Street Address:		
City:	State:	Zip Code:
Home Phone:	Cell Phone:	
Work Phone:	Email:	

Name:		
Street Address:		
City:	State:	Zip Code:
Home Phone:	Cell Phone:	
Work Phone:	Email:	

Name:		
Street Address:		
City:	State:	Zip Code:
Home Phone:	Cell Phone:	
Work Phone:	Email:	

J

Name:		
Street Address:		
City:	State:	Zip Code:
Home Phone:		Cell Phone:
Work Phone:		Email:

Name:		
Street Address:		
City:	State:	Zip Code:
Home Phone:		Cell Phone:
Work Phone:		Email:

Name:		
Street Address:		
City:	State:	Zip Code:
Home Phone:		Cell Phone:
Work Phone:		Email:

Name:		
Street Address:		
City:	State:	Zip Code:
Home Phone:		Cell Phone:
Work Phone:		Email:

Name:		
Street Address:		
City:	State:	Zip Code:
Home Phone:	Cell Phone:	
Work Phone:	Email:	

Name:		
Street Address:		
City:	State:	Zip Code:
Home Phone:	Cell Phone:	
Work Phone:	Email:	

Name:		
Street Address:		
City:	State:	Zip Code:
Home Phone:	Cell Phone:	
Work Phone:	Email:	

Name:		
Street Address:		
City:	State:	Zip Code:
Home Phone:	Cell Phone:	
Work Phone:	Email:	

J

Name:		
Street Address:		
City:	State:	Zip Code:
Home Phone:		Cell Phone:
Work Phone:		Email:

Name:		
Street Address:		
City:	State:	Zip Code:
Home Phone:		Cell Phone:
Work Phone:		Email:

Name:		
Street Address:		
City:	State:	Zip Code:
Home Phone:		Cell Phone:
Work Phone:		Email:

Name:		
Street Address:		
City:	State:	Zip Code:
Home Phone:		Cell Phone:
Work Phone:		Email:

K

Name:		
Street Address:		
City:	State:	Zip Code:
Home Phone:		Cell Phone:
Work Phone:		Email:

Name:		
Street Address:		
City:	State:	Zip Code:
Home Phone:		Cell Phone:
Work Phone:		Email:

Name:		
Street Address:		
City:	State:	Zip Code:
Home Phone:		Cell Phone:
Work Phone:		Email:

Name:		
Street Address:		
City:	State:	Zip Code:
Home Phone:		Cell Phone:
Work Phone:		Email:

K

Name:		
Street Address:		
City:	State:	Zip Code:
Home Phone:		Cell Phone:
Work Phone:		Email:

Name:		
Street Address:		
City:	State:	Zip Code:
Home Phone:		Cell Phone:
Work Phone:		Email:

Name:		
Street Address:		
City:	State:	Zip Code:
Home Phone:		Cell Phone:
Work Phone:		Email:

Name:		
Street Address:		
City:	State:	Zip Code:
Home Phone:		Cell Phone:
Work Phone:		Email:

K

Name:		
Street Address:		
City:	State:	Zip Code:
Home Phone:		Cell Phone:
Work Phone:		Email:

Name:		
Street Address:		
City:	State:	Zip Code:
Home Phone:		Cell Phone:
Work Phone:		Email:

Name:		
Street Address:		
City:	State:	Zip Code:
Home Phone:		Cell Phone:
Work Phone:		Email:

Name:		
Street Address:		
City:	State:	Zip Code:
Home Phone:		Cell Phone:
Work Phone:		Email:

K

<table>
<tr><td colspan="3">Name:</td></tr>
<tr><td colspan="3">Street Address:</td></tr>
<tr><td>City:</td><td>State:</td><td>Zip Code:</td></tr>
<tr><td colspan="2">Home Phone:</td><td>Cell Phone:</td></tr>
<tr><td colspan="2">Work Phone:</td><td>Email:</td></tr>
</table>

<table>
<tr><td colspan="3">Name:</td></tr>
<tr><td colspan="3">Street Address:</td></tr>
<tr><td>City:</td><td>State:</td><td>Zip Code:</td></tr>
<tr><td colspan="2">Home Phone:</td><td>Cell Phone:</td></tr>
<tr><td colspan="2">Work Phone:</td><td>Email:</td></tr>
</table>

<table>
<tr><td colspan="3">Name:</td></tr>
<tr><td colspan="3">Street Address:</td></tr>
<tr><td>City:</td><td>State:</td><td>Zip Code:</td></tr>
<tr><td colspan="2">Home Phone:</td><td>Cell Phone:</td></tr>
<tr><td colspan="2">Work Phone:</td><td>Email:</td></tr>
</table>

<table>
<tr><td colspan="3">Name:</td></tr>
<tr><td colspan="3">Street Address:</td></tr>
<tr><td>City:</td><td>State:</td><td>Zip Code:</td></tr>
<tr><td colspan="2">Home Phone:</td><td>Cell Phone:</td></tr>
<tr><td colspan="2">Work Phone:</td><td>Email:</td></tr>
</table>

Name:		
Street Address:		
City:	State:	Zip Code:
Home Phone:	Cell Phone:	
Work Phone:	Email:	

Name:		
Street Address:		
City:	State:	Zip Code:
Home Phone:	Cell Phone:	
Work Phone:	Email:	

Name:		
Street Address:		
City:	State:	Zip Code:
Home Phone:	Cell Phone:	
Work Phone:	Email:	

Name:		
Street Address:		
City:	State:	Zip Code:
Home Phone:	Cell Phone:	
Work Phone:	Email:	

K

Name:		
Street Address:		
City:	State:	Zip Code:
Home Phone:		Cell Phone:
Work Phone:		Email:

Name:		
Street Address:		
City:	State:	Zip Code:
Home Phone:		Cell Phone:
Work Phone:		Email:

Name:		
Street Address:		
City:	State:	Zip Code:
Home Phone:		Cell Phone:
Work Phone:		Email:

Name:		
Street Address:		
City:	State:	Zip Code:
Home Phone:		Cell Phone:
Work Phone:		Email:

L

Name:		
Street Address:		
City:	State:	Zip Code:
Home Phone:		Cell Phone:
Work Phone:		Email:

Name:		
Street Address:		
City:	State:	Zip Code:
Home Phone:		Cell Phone:
Work Phone:		Email:

Name:		
Street Address:		
City:	State:	Zip Code:
Home Phone:		Cell Phone:
Work Phone:		Email:

Name:		
Street Address:		
City:	State:	Zip Code:
Home Phone:		Cell Phone:
Work Phone:		Email:

L

Name:		
Street Address:		
City:	State:	Zip Code:
Home Phone:		Cell Phone:
Work Phone:		Email:

Name:		
Street Address:		
City:	State:	Zip Code:
Home Phone:		Cell Phone:
Work Phone:		Email:

Name:		
Street Address:		
City:	State:	Zip Code:
Home Phone:		Cell Phone:
Work Phone:		Email:

Name:		
Street Address:		
City:	State:	Zip Code:
Home Phone:		Cell Phone:
Work Phone:		Email:

L

Name:
Street Address:

City:	State:	Zip Code:

Home Phone:	Cell Phone:
Work Phone:	Email:

Name:
Street Address:

City:	State:	Zip Code:

Home Phone:	Cell Phone:
Work Phone:	Email:

Name:
Street Address:

City:	State:	Zip Code:

Home Phone:	Cell Phone:
Work Phone:	Email:

Name:
Street Address:

City:	State:	Zip Code:

Home Phone:	Cell Phone:
Work Phone:	Email:

L

Name:		
Street Address:		
City:	State:	Zip Code:
Home Phone:		Cell Phone:
Work Phone:		Email:

Name:		
Street Address:		
City:	State:	Zip Code:
Home Phone:		Cell Phone:
Work Phone:		Email:

Name:		
Street Address:		
City:	State:	Zip Code:
Home Phone:		Cell Phone:
Work Phone:		Email:

Name:		
Street Address:		
City:	State:	Zip Code:
Home Phone:		Cell Phone:
Work Phone:		Email:

M

Name:		
Street Address:		
City:	State:	Zip Code:
Home Phone:	Cell Phone:	
Work Phone:	Email:	

Name:		
Street Address:		
City:	State:	Zip Code:
Home Phone:	Cell Phone:	
Work Phone:	Email:	

Name:		
Street Address:		
City:	State:	Zip Code:
Home Phone:	Cell Phone:	
Work Phone:	Email:	

Name:		
Street Address:		
City:	State:	Zip Code:
Home Phone:	Cell Phone:	
Work Phone:	Email:	

M

Name:		
Street Address:		
City:	State:	Zip Code:
Home Phone:		Cell Phone:
Work Phone:		Email:

Name:		
Street Address:		
City:	State:	Zip Code:
Home Phone:		Cell Phone:
Work Phone:		Email:

Name:		
Street Address:		
City:	State:	Zip Code:
Home Phone:		Cell Phone:
Work Phone:		Email:

Name:		
Street Address:		
City:	State:	Zip Code:
Home Phone:		Cell Phone:
Work Phone:		Email:

Name:		
Street Address:		
City:	State:	Zip Code:
Home Phone:	Cell Phone:	
Work Phone:	Email:	

Name:		
Street Address:		
City:	State:	Zip Code:
Home Phone:	Cell Phone:	
Work Phone:	Email:	

Name:		
Street Address:		
City:	State:	Zip Code:
Home Phone:	Cell Phone:	
Work Phone:	Email:	

Name:		
Street Address:		
City:	State:	Zip Code:
Home Phone:	Cell Phone:	
Work Phone:	Email:	

M

Name:		
Street Address:		
City:	State:	Zip Code:
Home Phone:		Cell Phone:
Work Phone:		Email:

Name:		
Street Address:		
City:	State:	Zip Code:
Home Phone:		Cell Phone:
Work Phone:		Email:

Name:		
Street Address:		
City:	State:	Zip Code:
Home Phone:		Cell Phone:
Work Phone:		Email:

Name:		
Street Address:		
City:	State:	Zip Code:
Home Phone:		Cell Phone:
Work Phone:		Email:

Name:		
Street Address:		
City:	State:	Zip Code:
Home Phone:	Cell Phone:	
Work Phone:	Email:	

Name:		
Street Address:		
City:	State:	Zip Code:
Home Phone:	Cell Phone:	
Work Phone:	Email:	

Name:		
Street Address:		
City:	State:	Zip Code:
Home Phone:	Cell Phone:	
Work Phone:	Email:	

Name:		
Street Address:		
City:	State:	Zip Code:
Home Phone:	Cell Phone:	
Work Phone:	Email:	

M

Name:		
Street Address:		
City:	State:	Zip Code:
Home Phone:		Cell Phone:
Work Phone:		Email:

Name:		
Street Address:		
City:	State:	Zip Code:
Home Phone:		Cell Phone:
Work Phone:		Email:

Name:		
Street Address:		
City:	State:	Zip Code:
Home Phone:		Cell Phone:
Work Phone:		Email:

Name:		
Street Address:		
City:	State:	Zip Code:
Home Phone:		Cell Phone:
Work Phone:		Email:

Name:		
Street Address:		
City:	State:	Zip Code:
Home Phone:		Cell Phone:
Work Phone:		Email:

Name:		
Street Address:		
City:	State:	Zip Code:
Home Phone:		Cell Phone:
Work Phone:		Email:

Name:		
Street Address:		
City:	State:	Zip Code:
Home Phone:		Cell Phone:
Work Phone:		Email:

Name:		
Street Address:		
City:	State:	Zip Code:
Home Phone:		Cell Phone:
Work Phone:		Email:

N

Name:		
Street Address:		
City:	State:	Zip Code:
Home Phone:		Cell Phone:
Work Phone:		Email:

Name:		
Street Address:		
City:	State:	Zip Code:
Home Phone:		Cell Phone:
Work Phone:		Email:

Name:		
Street Address:		
City:	State:	Zip Code:
Home Phone:		Cell Phone:
Work Phone:		Email:

Name:		
Street Address:		
City:	State:	Zip Code:
Home Phone:		Cell Phone:
Work Phone:		Email:

Name:		
Street Address:		
City:	State:	Zip Code:
Home Phone:		Cell Phone:
Work Phone:		Email:

Name:		
Street Address:		
City:	State:	Zip Code:
Home Phone:		Cell Phone:
Work Phone:		Email:

Name:		
Street Address:		
City:	State:	Zip Code:
Home Phone:		Cell Phone:
Work Phone:		Email:

Name:		
Street Address:		
City:	State:	Zip Code:
Home Phone:		Cell Phone:
Work Phone:		Email:

N

Name:		
Street Address:		
City:	State:	Zip Code:
Home Phone:		Cell Phone:
Work Phone:		Email:

Name:		
Street Address:		
City:	State:	Zip Code:
Home Phone:		Cell Phone:
Work Phone:		Email:

Name:		
Street Address:		
City:	State:	Zip Code:
Home Phone:		Cell Phone:
Work Phone:		Email:

Name:		
Street Address:		
City:	State:	Zip Code:
Home Phone:		Cell Phone:
Work Phone:		Email:

O

Name:		
Street Address:		
City:	State:	Zip Code:
Home Phone:		Cell Phone:
Work Phone:		Email:

Name:		
Street Address:		
City:	State:	Zip Code:
Home Phone:		Cell Phone:
Work Phone:		Email:

Name:		
Street Address:		
City:	State:	Zip Code:
Home Phone:		Cell Phone:
Work Phone:		Email:

Name:		
Street Address:		
City:	State:	Zip Code:
Home Phone:		Cell Phone:
Work Phone:		Email:

O

Name:		
Street Address:		
City:	State:	Zip Code:
Home Phone:		Cell Phone:
Work Phone:		Email:

Name:		
Street Address:		
City:	State:	Zip Code:
Home Phone:		Cell Phone:
Work Phone:		Email:

Name:		
Street Address:		
City:	State:	Zip Code:
Home Phone:		Cell Phone:
Work Phone:		Email:

Name:		
Street Address:		
City:	State:	Zip Code:
Home Phone:		Cell Phone:
Work Phone:		Email:

Name:		
Street Address:		
City:	State:	Zip Code:
Home Phone:		Cell Phone:
Work Phone:		Email:

Name:		
Street Address:		
City:	State:	Zip Code:
Home Phone:		Cell Phone:
Work Phone:		Email:

Name:		
Street Address:		
City:	State:	Zip Code:
Home Phone:		Cell Phone:
Work Phone:		Email:

Name:		
Street Address:		
City:	State:	Zip Code:
Home Phone:		Cell Phone:
Work Phone:		Email:

O

Name:		
Street Address:		
City:	State:	Zip Code:
Home Phone:		Cell Phone:
Work Phone:		Email:

Name:		
Street Address:		
City:	State:	Zip Code:
Home Phone:		Cell Phone:
Work Phone:		Email:

Name:		
Street Address:		
City:	State:	Zip Code:
Home Phone:		Cell Phone:
Work Phone:		Email:

Name:		
Street Address:		
City:	State:	Zip Code:
Home Phone:		Cell Phone:
Work Phone:		Email:

Name:		
Street Address:		
City:	State:	Zip Code:
Home Phone:	Cell Phone:	
Work Phone:	Email:	

Name:		
Street Address:		
City:	State:	Zip Code:
Home Phone:	Cell Phone:	
Work Phone:	Email:	

Name:		
Street Address:		
City:	State:	Zip Code:
Home Phone:	Cell Phone:	
Work Phone:	Email:	

Name:		
Street Address:		
City:	State:	Zip Code:
Home Phone:	Cell Phone:	
Work Phone:	Email:	

P

Name:		
Street Address:		
City:	State:	Zip Code:
Home Phone:		Cell Phone:
Work Phone:		Email:

Name:		
Street Address:		
City:	State:	Zip Code:
Home Phone:		Cell Phone:
Work Phone:		Email:

Name:		
Street Address:		
City:	State:	Zip Code:
Home Phone:		Cell Phone:
Work Phone:		Email:

Name:		
Street Address:		
City:	State:	Zip Code:
Home Phone:		Cell Phone:
Work Phone:		Email:

Name:		
Street Address:		
City:	State:	Zip Code:
Home Phone:	Cell Phone:	
Work Phone:	Email:	

Name:		
Street Address:		
City:	State:	Zip Code:
Home Phone:	Cell Phone:	
Work Phone:	Email:	

Name:		
Street Address:		
City:	State:	Zip Code:
Home Phone:	Cell Phone:	
Work Phone:	Email:	

Name:		
Street Address:		
City:	State:	Zip Code:
Home Phone:	Cell Phone:	
Work Phone:	Email:	

P

Name:		
Street Address:		
City:	State:	Zip Code:
Home Phone:		Cell Phone:
Work Phone:		Email:

Name:		
Street Address:		
City:	State:	Zip Code:
Home Phone:		Cell Phone:
Work Phone:		Email:

Name:		
Street Address:		
City:	State:	Zip Code:
Home Phone:		Cell Phone:
Work Phone:		Email:

Name:		
Street Address:		
City:	State:	Zip Code:
Home Phone:		Cell Phone:
Work Phone:		Email:

Q

Name:		
Street Address:		
City:	State:	Zip Code:
Home Phone:		Cell Phone:
Work Phone:		Email:

Name:		
Street Address:		
City:	State:	Zip Code:
Home Phone:		Cell Phone:
Work Phone:		Email:

Name:		
Street Address:		
City:	State:	Zip Code:
Home Phone:		Cell Phone:
Work Phone:		Email:

Name:		
Street Address:		
City:	State:	Zip Code:
Home Phone:		Cell Phone:
Work Phone:		Email:

Q

Name:		
Street Address:		
City:	State:	Zip Code:
Home Phone:		Cell Phone:
Work Phone:		Email:

Name:		
Street Address:		
City:	State:	Zip Code:
Home Phone:		Cell Phone:
Work Phone:		Email:

Name:		
Street Address:		
City:	State:	Zip Code:
Home Phone:		Cell Phone:
Work Phone:		Email:

Name:		
Street Address:		
City:	State:	Zip Code:
Home Phone:		Cell Phone:
Work Phone:		Email:

Q

Name:		
Street Address:		
City:	State:	Zip Code:
Home Phone:		Cell Phone:
Work Phone:		Email:

Name:		
Street Address:		
City:	State:	Zip Code:
Home Phone:		Cell Phone:
Work Phone:		Email:

Name:		
Street Address:		
City:	State:	Zip Code:
Home Phone:		Cell Phone:
Work Phone:		Email:

Name:		
Street Address:		
City:	State:	Zip Code:
Home Phone:		Cell Phone:
Work Phone:		Email:

Q

Name:		
Street Address:		
City:	State:	Zip Code:
Home Phone:		Cell Phone:
Work Phone:		Email:

Name:		
Street Address:		
City:	State:	Zip Code:
Home Phone:		Cell Phone:
Work Phone:		Email:

Name:		
Street Address:		
City:	State:	Zip Code:
Home Phone:		Cell Phone:
Work Phone:		Email:

Name:		
Street Address:		
City:	State:	Zip Code:
Home Phone:		Cell Phone:
Work Phone:		Email:

R

Name:		
Street Address:		
City:	State:	Zip Code:
Home Phone:		Cell Phone:
Work Phone:		Email:

Name:		
Street Address:		
City:	State:	Zip Code:
Home Phone:		Cell Phone:
Work Phone:		Email:

Name:		
Street Address:		
City:	State:	Zip Code:
Home Phone:		Cell Phone:
Work Phone:		Email:

Name:		
Street Address:		
City:	State:	Zip Code:
Home Phone:		Cell Phone:
Work Phone:		Email:

R

Name:		
Street Address:		
City:	State:	Zip Code:
Home Phone:		Cell Phone:
Work Phone:		Email:

Name:		
Street Address:		
City:	State:	Zip Code:
Home Phone:		Cell Phone:
Work Phone:		Email:

Name:		
Street Address:		
City:	State:	Zip Code:
Home Phone:		Cell Phone:
Work Phone:		Email:

Name:		
Street Address:		
City:	State:	Zip Code:
Home Phone:		Cell Phone:
Work Phone:		Email:

Name:		
Street Address:		
City:	State:	Zip Code:
Home Phone:		Cell Phone:
Work Phone:		Email:

Name:		
Street Address:		
City:	State:	Zip Code:
Home Phone:		Cell Phone:
Work Phone:		Email:

Name:		
Street Address:		
City:	State:	Zip Code:
Home Phone:		Cell Phone:
Work Phone:		Email:

Name:		
Street Address:		
City:	State:	Zip Code:
Home Phone:		Cell Phone:
Work Phone:		Email:

R

Name:		
Street Address:		
City:	State:	Zip Code:
Home Phone:	Cell Phone:	
Work Phone:	Email:	

Name:		
Street Address:		
City:	State:	Zip Code:
Home Phone:	Cell Phone:	
Work Phone:	Email:	

Name:		
Street Address:		
City:	State:	Zip Code:
Home Phone:	Cell Phone:	
Work Phone:	Email:	

Name:		
Street Address:		
City:	State:	Zip Code:
Home Phone:	Cell Phone:	
Work Phone:	Email:	

Name:		
Street Address:		
City:	State:	Zip Code:
Home Phone:		Cell Phone:
Work Phone:		Email:

Name:		
Street Address:		
City:	State:	Zip Code:
Home Phone:		Cell Phone:
Work Phone:		Email:

Name:		
Street Address:		
City:	State:	Zip Code:
Home Phone:		Cell Phone:
Work Phone:		Email:

Name:		
Street Address:		
City:	State:	Zip Code:
Home Phone:		Cell Phone:
Work Phone:		Email:

S

Name:		
Street Address:		
City:	State:	Zip Code:
Home Phone:	Cell Phone:	
Work Phone:	Email:	

Name:		
Street Address:		
City:	State:	Zip Code:
Home Phone:	Cell Phone:	
Work Phone:	Email:	

Name:		
Street Address:		
City:	State:	Zip Code:
Home Phone:	Cell Phone:	
Work Phone:	Email:	

Name:		
Street Address:		
City:	State:	Zip Code:
Home Phone:	Cell Phone:	
Work Phone:	Email:	

S

Name:		
Street Address:		
City:	State:	Zip Code:
Home Phone:		Cell Phone:
Work Phone:		Email:

Name:		
Street Address:		
City:	State:	Zip Code:
Home Phone:		Cell Phone:
Work Phone:		Email:

Name:		
Street Address:		
City:	State:	Zip Code:
Home Phone:		Cell Phone:
Work Phone:		Email:

Name:		
Street Address:		
City:	State:	Zip Code:
Home Phone:		Cell Phone:
Work Phone:		Email:

S

Name:		
Street Address:		
City:	State:	Zip Code:
Home Phone:		Cell Phone:
Work Phone:		Email:

Name:		
Street Address:		
City:	State:	Zip Code:
Home Phone:		Cell Phone:
Work Phone:		Email:

Name:		
Street Address:		
City:	State:	Zip Code:
Home Phone:		Cell Phone:
Work Phone:		Email:

Name:		
Street Address:		
City:	State:	Zip Code:
Home Phone:		Cell Phone:
Work Phone:		Email:

T

Name:		
Street Address:		
City:	State:	Zip Code:
Home Phone:		Cell Phone:
Work Phone:		Email:

Name:		
Street Address:		
City:	State:	Zip Code:
Home Phone:		Cell Phone:
Work Phone:		Email:

Name:		
Street Address:		
City:	State:	Zip Code:
Home Phone:		Cell Phone:
Work Phone:		Email:

Name:		
Street Address:		
City:	State:	Zip Code:
Home Phone:		Cell Phone:
Work Phone:		Email:

T

Name:		
Street Address:		
City:	State:	Zip Code:
Home Phone:		Cell Phone:
Work Phone:		Email:

Name:		
Street Address:		
City:	State:	Zip Code:
Home Phone:		Cell Phone:
Work Phone:		Email:

Name:		
Street Address:		
City:	State:	Zip Code:
Home Phone:		Cell Phone:
Work Phone:		Email:

Name:		
Street Address:		
City:	State:	Zip Code:
Home Phone:		Cell Phone:
Work Phone:		Email:

Name:		
Street Address:		
City:	State:	Zip Code:
Home Phone:	Cell Phone:	
Work Phone:	Email:	

Name:		
Street Address:		
City:	State:	Zip Code:
Home Phone:	Cell Phone:	
Work Phone:	Email:	

Name:		
Street Address:		
City:	State:	Zip Code:
Home Phone:	Cell Phone:	
Work Phone:	Email:	

Name:		
Street Address:		
City:	State:	Zip Code:
Home Phone:	Cell Phone:	
Work Phone:	Email:	

T

Name:
Street Address:

City:	State:	Zip Code:

Home Phone:	Cell Phone:
Work Phone:	Email:

Name:
Street Address:

City:	State:	Zip Code:

Home Phone:	Cell Phone:
Work Phone:	Email:

Name:
Street Address:

City:	State:	Zip Code:

Home Phone:	Cell Phone:
Work Phone:	Email:

Name:
Street Address:

City:	State:	Zip Code:

Home Phone:	Cell Phone:
Work Phone:	Email:

T

Name:		
Street Address:		
City:	State:	Zip Code:
Home Phone:		Cell Phone:
Work Phone:		Email:

Name:		
Street Address:		
City:	State:	Zip Code:
Home Phone:		Cell Phone:
Work Phone:		Email:

Name:		
Street Address:		
City:	State:	Zip Code:
Home Phone:		Cell Phone:
Work Phone:		Email:

Name:		
Street Address:		
City:	State:	Zip Code:
Home Phone:		Cell Phone:
Work Phone:		Email:

T

Name:		
Street Address:		
City:	State:	Zip Code:
Home Phone:		Cell Phone:
Work Phone:		Email:

Name:		
Street Address:		
City:	State:	Zip Code:
Home Phone:		Cell Phone:
Work Phone:		Email:

Name:		
Street Address:		
City:	State:	Zip Code:
Home Phone:		Cell Phone:
Work Phone:		Email:

Name:		
Street Address:		
City:	State:	Zip Code:
Home Phone:		Cell Phone:
Work Phone:		Email:

Name:		
Street Address:		
City:	State:	Zip Code:
Home Phone:		Cell Phone:
Work Phone:		Email:

Name:		
Street Address:		
City:	State:	Zip Code:
Home Phone:		Cell Phone:
Work Phone:		Email:

Name:		
Street Address:		
City:	State:	Zip Code:
Home Phone:		Cell Phone:
Work Phone:		Email:

Name:		
Street Address:		
City:	State:	Zip Code:
Home Phone:		Cell Phone:
Work Phone:		Email:

U

Name:		
Street Address:		
City:	State:	Zip Code:
Home Phone:		Cell Phone:
Work Phone:		Email:

Name:		
Street Address:		
City:	State:	Zip Code:
Home Phone:		Cell Phone:
Work Phone:		Email:

Name:		
Street Address:		
City:	State:	Zip Code:
Home Phone:		Cell Phone:
Work Phone:		Email:

Name:		
Street Address:		
City:	State:	Zip Code:
Home Phone:		Cell Phone:
Work Phone:		Email:

Name:		
Street Address:		
City:	State:	Zip Code:
Home Phone:		Cell Phone:
Work Phone:		Email:

Name:		
Street Address:		
City:	State:	Zip Code:
Home Phone:		Cell Phone:
Work Phone:		Email:

Name:		
Street Address:		
City:	State:	Zip Code:
Home Phone:		Cell Phone:
Work Phone:		Email:

Name:		
Street Address:		
City:	State:	Zip Code:
Home Phone:		Cell Phone:
Work Phone:		Email:

U

Name:		
Street Address:		
City:	State:	Zip Code:
Home Phone:		Cell Phone:
Work Phone:		Email:

Name:		
Street Address:		
City:	State:	Zip Code:
Home Phone:		Cell Phone:
Work Phone:		Email:

Name:		
Street Address:		
City:	State:	Zip Code:
Home Phone:		Cell Phone:
Work Phone:		Email:

Name:		
Street Address:		
City:	State:	Zip Code:
Home Phone:		Cell Phone:
Work Phone:		Email:

U

Name:		
Street Address:		
City:	State:	Zip Code:
Home Phone:		Cell Phone:
Work Phone:		Email:

Name:		
Street Address:		
City:	State:	Zip Code:
Home Phone:		Cell Phone:
Work Phone:		Email:

Name:		
Street Address:		
City:	State:	Zip Code:
Home Phone:		Cell Phone:
Work Phone:		Email:

Name:		
Street Address:		
City:	State:	Zip Code:
Home Phone:		Cell Phone:
Work Phone:		Email:

U

Name:		
Street Address:		
City:	State:	Zip Code:
Home Phone:		Cell Phone:
Work Phone:		Email:

Name:		
Street Address:		
City:	State:	Zip Code:
Home Phone:		Cell Phone:
Work Phone:		Email:

Name:		
Street Address:		
City:	State:	Zip Code:
Home Phone:		Cell Phone:
Work Phone:		Email:

Name:		
Street Address:		
City:	State:	Zip Code:
Home Phone:		Cell Phone:
Work Phone:		Email:

Name:		
Street Address:		
City:	State:	Zip Code:
Home Phone:		Cell Phone:
Work Phone:		Email:

Name:		
Street Address:		
City:	State:	Zip Code:
Home Phone:		Cell Phone:
Work Phone:		Email:

Name:		
Street Address:		
City:	State:	Zip Code:
Home Phone:		Cell Phone:
Work Phone:		Email:

Name:		
Street Address:		
City:	State:	Zip Code:
Home Phone:		Cell Phone:
Work Phone:		Email:

V

Name:		
Street Address:		
City:	State:	Zip Code:
Home Phone:	Cell Phone:	
Work Phone:	Email:	

Name:		
Street Address:		
City:	State:	Zip Code:
Home Phone:	Cell Phone:	
Work Phone:	Email:	

Name:		
Street Address:		
City:	State:	Zip Code:
Home Phone:	Cell Phone:	
Work Phone:	Email:	

Name:		
Street Address:		
City:	State:	Zip Code:
Home Phone:	Cell Phone:	
Work Phone:	Email:	

V

Name:		
Street Address:		
City:	State:	Zip Code:
Home Phone:		Cell Phone:
Work Phone:		Email:

Name:		
Street Address:		
City:	State:	Zip Code:
Home Phone:		Cell Phone:
Work Phone:		Email:

Name:		
Street Address:		
City:	State:	Zip Code:
Home Phone:		Cell Phone:
Work Phone:		Email:

Name:		
Street Address:		
City:	State:	Zip Code:
Home Phone:		Cell Phone:
Work Phone:		Email:

V

Name:		
Street Address:		
City:	State:	Zip Code:
Home Phone:		Cell Phone:
Work Phone:		Email:

Name:		
Street Address:		
City:	State:	Zip Code:
Home Phone:		Cell Phone:
Work Phone:		Email:

Name:		
Street Address:		
City:	State:	Zip Code:
Home Phone:		Cell Phone:
Work Phone:		Email:

Name:		
Street Address:		
City:	State:	Zip Code:
Home Phone:		Cell Phone:
Work Phone:		Email:

W

Name:		
Street Address:		
City:	State:	Zip Code:
Home Phone:		Cell Phone:
Work Phone:		Email:

Name:		
Street Address:		
City:	State:	Zip Code:
Home Phone:		Cell Phone:
Work Phone:		Email:

Name:		
Street Address:		
City:	State:	Zip Code:
Home Phone:		Cell Phone:
Work Phone:		Email:

Name:		
Street Address:		
City:	State:	Zip Code:
Home Phone:		Cell Phone:
Work Phone:		Email:

W

Name:		
Street Address:		
City:	State:	Zip Code:
Home Phone:		Cell Phone:
Work Phone:		Email:

Name:		
Street Address:		
City:	State:	Zip Code:
Home Phone:		Cell Phone:
Work Phone:		Email:

Name:		
Street Address:		
City:	State:	Zip Code:
Home Phone:		Cell Phone:
Work Phone:		Email:

Name:		
Street Address:		
City:	State:	Zip Code:
Home Phone:		Cell Phone:
Work Phone:		Email:

Name:		
Street Address:		
City:	State:	Zip Code:
Home Phone:		Cell Phone:
Work Phone:		Email:

Name:		
Street Address:		
City:	State:	Zip Code:
Home Phone:		Cell Phone:
Work Phone:		Email:

Name:		
Street Address:		
City:	State:	Zip Code:
Home Phone:		Cell Phone:
Work Phone:		Email:

Name:		
Street Address:		
City:	State:	Zip Code:
Home Phone:		Cell Phone:
Work Phone:		Email:

W

Name:		
Street Address:		
City:	State:	Zip Code:
Home Phone:		Cell Phone:
Work Phone:		Email:

Name:		
Street Address:		
City:	State:	Zip Code:
Home Phone:		Cell Phone:
Work Phone:		Email:

Name:		
Street Address:		
City:	State:	Zip Code:
Home Phone:		Cell Phone:
Work Phone:		Email:

Name:		
Street Address:		
City:	State:	Zip Code:
Home Phone:		Cell Phone:
Work Phone:		Email:

W

Name:		
Street Address:		
City:	State:	Zip Code:
Home Phone:		Cell Phone:
Work Phone:		Email:

Name:		
Street Address:		
City:	State:	Zip Code:
Home Phone:		Cell Phone:
Work Phone:		Email:

Name:		
Street Address:		
City:	State:	Zip Code:
Home Phone:		Cell Phone:
Work Phone:		Email:

Name:		
Street Address:		
City:	State:	Zip Code:
Home Phone:		Cell Phone:
Work Phone:		Email:

W

Name:		
Street Address:		
City:	State:	Zip Code:
Home Phone:		Cell Phone:
Work Phone:		Email:

Name:		
Street Address:		
City:	State:	Zip Code:
Home Phone:		Cell Phone:
Work Phone:		Email:

Name:		
Street Address:		
City:	State:	Zip Code:
Home Phone:		Cell Phone:
Work Phone:		Email:

Name:		
Street Address:		
City:	State:	Zip Code:
Home Phone:		Cell Phone:
Work Phone:		Email:

X

Name:		
Street Address:		
City:	State:	Zip Code:
Home Phone:		Cell Phone:
Work Phone:		Email:

Name:		
Street Address:		
City:	State:	Zip Code:
Home Phone:		Cell Phone:
Work Phone:		Email:

Name:		
Street Address:		
City:	State:	Zip Code:
Home Phone:		Cell Phone:
Work Phone:		Email:

Name:		
Street Address:		
City:	State:	Zip Code:
Home Phone:		Cell Phone:
Work Phone:		Email:

X

Name:		
Street Address:		
City:	State:	Zip Code:
Home Phone:		Cell Phone:
Work Phone:		Email:

Name:		
Street Address:		
City:	State:	Zip Code:
Home Phone:		Cell Phone:
Work Phone:		Email:

Name:		
Street Address:		
City:	State:	Zip Code:
Home Phone:		Cell Phone:
Work Phone:		Email:

Name:		
Street Address:		
City:	State:	Zip Code:
Home Phone:		Cell Phone:
Work Phone:		Email:

X

Name:		
Street Address:		
City:	State:	Zip Code:
Home Phone:		Cell Phone:
Work Phone:		Email:

Name:		
Street Address:		
City:	State:	Zip Code:
Home Phone:		Cell Phone:
Work Phone:		Email:

Name:		
Street Address:		
City:	State:	Zip Code:
Home Phone:		Cell Phone:
Work Phone:		Email:

Name:		
Street Address:		
City:	State:	Zip Code:
Home Phone:		Cell Phone:
Work Phone:		Email:

X

Name:		
Street Address:		
City:	State:	Zip Code:
Home Phone:		Cell Phone:
Work Phone:		Email:

Name:		
Street Address:		
City:	State:	Zip Code:
Home Phone:		Cell Phone:
Work Phone:		Email:

Name:		
Street Address:		
City:	State:	Zip Code:
Home Phone:		Cell Phone:
Work Phone:		Email:

Name:		
Street Address:		
City:	State:	Zip Code:
Home Phone:		Cell Phone:
Work Phone:		Email:

Y

Name:		
Street Address:		
City:	State:	Zip Code:
Home Phone:		Cell Phone:
Work Phone:		Email:

Name:		
Street Address:		
City:	State:	Zip Code:
Home Phone:		Cell Phone:
Work Phone:		Email:

Name:		
Street Address:		
City:	State:	Zip Code:
Home Phone:		Cell Phone:
Work Phone:		Email:

Name:		
Street Address:		
City:	State:	Zip Code:
Home Phone:		Cell Phone:
Work Phone:		Email:

Y

Name:		
Street Address:		
City:	State:	Zip Code:
Home Phone:		Cell Phone:
Work Phone:		Email:

Name:		
Street Address:		
City:	State:	Zip Code:
Home Phone:		Cell Phone:
Work Phone:		Email:

Name:		
Street Address:		
City:	State:	Zip Code:
Home Phone:		Cell Phone:
Work Phone:		Email:

Name:		
Street Address:		
City:	State:	Zip Code:
Home Phone:		Cell Phone:
Work Phone:		Email:

Y

Name:		
Street Address:		
City:	State:	Zip Code:
Home Phone:		Cell Phone:
Work Phone:		Email:

Name:		
Street Address:		
City:	State:	Zip Code:
Home Phone:		Cell Phone:
Work Phone:		Email:

Name:		
Street Address:		
City:	State:	Zip Code:
Home Phone:		Cell Phone:
Work Phone:		Email:

Name:		
Street Address:		
City:	State:	Zip Code:
Home Phone:		Cell Phone:
Work Phone:		Email:

Y

Name:		
Street Address:		
City:	State:	Zip Code:
Home Phone:		Cell Phone:
Work Phone:		Email:

Name:		
Street Address:		
City:	State:	Zip Code:
Home Phone:		Cell Phone:
Work Phone:		Email:

Name:		
Street Address:		
City:	State:	Zip Code:
Home Phone:		Cell Phone:
Work Phone:		Email:

Name:		
Street Address:		
City:	State:	Zip Code:
Home Phone:		Cell Phone:
Work Phone:		Email:

Y

Name:		
Street Address:		
City:	State:	Zip Code:
Home Phone:		Cell Phone:
Work Phone:		Email:

Name:		
Street Address:		
City:	State:	Zip Code:
Home Phone:		Cell Phone:
Work Phone:		Email:

Name:		
Street Address:		
City:	State:	Zip Code:
Home Phone:		Cell Phone:
Work Phone:		Email:

Name:		
Street Address:		
City:	State:	Zip Code:
Home Phone:		Cell Phone:
Work Phone:		Email:

Y

Name:		
Street Address:		
City:	State:	Zip Code:
Home Phone:		Cell Phone:
Work Phone:		Email:

Name:		
Street Address:		
City:	State:	Zip Code:
Home Phone:		Cell Phone:
Work Phone:		Email:

Name:		
Street Address:		
City:	State:	Zip Code:
Home Phone:		Cell Phone:
Work Phone:		Email:

Name:		
Street Address:		
City:	State:	Zip Code:
Home Phone:		Cell Phone:
Work Phone:		Email:

Name:		
Street Address:		
City:	State:	Zip Code:
Home Phone:		Cell Phone:
Work Phone:		Email:

Name:		
Street Address:		
City:	State:	Zip Code:
Home Phone:		Cell Phone:
Work Phone:		Email:

Name:		
Street Address:		
City:	State:	Zip Code:
Home Phone:		Cell Phone:
Work Phone:		Email:

Name:		
Street Address:		
City:	State:	Zip Code:
Home Phone:		Cell Phone:
Work Phone:		Email:

Z

Name:		
Street Address:		
City:	State:	Zip Code:
Home Phone:		Cell Phone:
Work Phone:		Email:

Name:		
Street Address:		
City:	State:	Zip Code:
Home Phone:		Cell Phone:
Work Phone:		Email:

Name:		
Street Address:		
City:	State:	Zip Code:
Home Phone:		Cell Phone:
Work Phone:		Email:

Name:		
Street Address:		
City:	State:	Zip Code:
Home Phone:		Cell Phone:
Work Phone:		Email:

NOTES

NOTES

NOTES

NOTES